Level 2
Activity Book 8

GW00733323

1 Complete each word.

c__t

b__s

s___ck

d__g

t__n

d__ck

s__x

f__n

f__sh

2 Join each word to a picture.

table

chair

plate

food

band

people

3 Trace and copy.

Come here!

The dinosaur egg

1 Join each word to a picture.

bed

baby

red

dinosaur

nest

green

2 Add **ing** to each word.

do____   roll____

crack____   bang____

jump____   break____

ABC Reading eggs

3 Draw a line under the correct sentence.

The egg is green.
The egg is red.

This is a dragon.
This is a dinosaur.

The girl is in bed.
The boy is in bed.

The egg is cracking.
The dog is cracking.

Hello baby dinosaur!
Hello little cat!

Meg the hen

1 Match each picture to a word.

book

egg

ten

bell

hen

pen

2 Find the matching pairs.

Wednesday

Sunday

Tuesday

Tuesday

Monday

Wednesday

Friday

Thursday

Sunday

Monday

Saturday

Friday

Saturday

Thursday

3 Match each sentence to a picture.

On Monday,
Meg the Hen lays ten eggs.

On Tuesday,
Meg looks at a book.

On Wednesday,
Meg gets ten little, red beds.

On Thursday,
Meg gets ten red pens.

On Friday,
Meg gets ten little bells.

On Saturday,
Meg has a rest.

On Sunday,
The ten eggs crack and open.

Fun spot 1

1 Complete the dot-to-dot.

2 Circle the things that can:

roll

jump

fly

swim

1 **Power words.** Join each word to a picture.

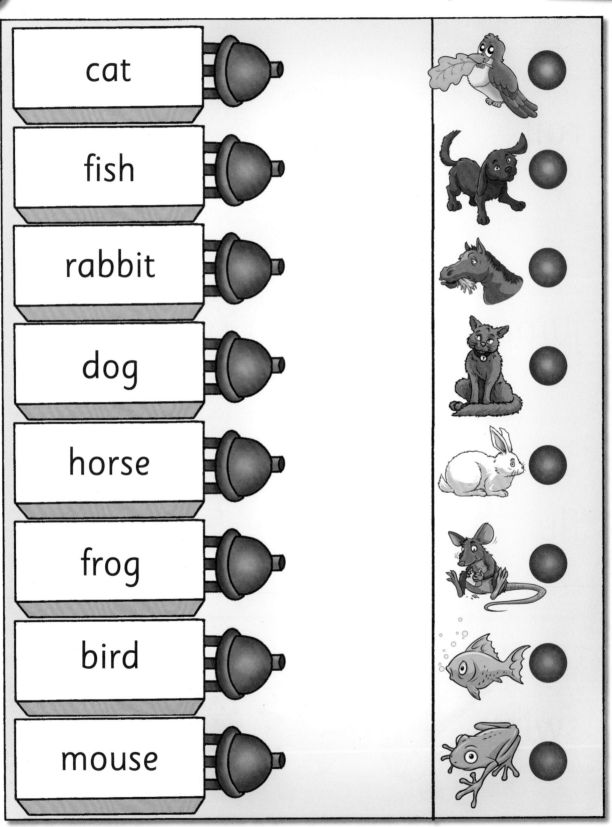

cat

fish

rabbit

dog

horse

frog

bird

mouse

rabbit.
dog.
cat.
frog.

3 Complete each sentence.

My pet is a

_____

_____

My pet is a

_____

_____

My pet is a

_____

_____

My pet is a

_____

_____

1 Match each sentence to a picture.

Where you can sleep.

Where you can play.

Where you can eat.

Where you can climb.

2 Trace and copy.

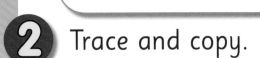

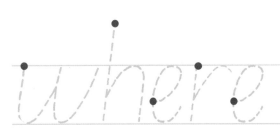

Where
When

3 Complete each question.

is Jazz the Cat going?

is Sam the Ant going?

is Sid the Kid going?

are you all coming down?
Now! Now! Now!

Fun spot 2

1

Find 2 Meg the Hens.

Find 3 Big Bens.

Find 6 Jet Sets.

Find 4 Eggsters.

2 Please recycle! Put things into the correct bin.

Paper and Cardboard

Cans

Plastic

1 Match each picture to a word.

pen

egg

peg

hen

leg

ten

2 Write each word.

ABC
Reading
eggs

2 Complete each sentence.

Ben has _legs_.

A hen has _____

Five _____

An egg on legs in a

_____

They get into _____

1 **Power words.** Join each word to a picture.

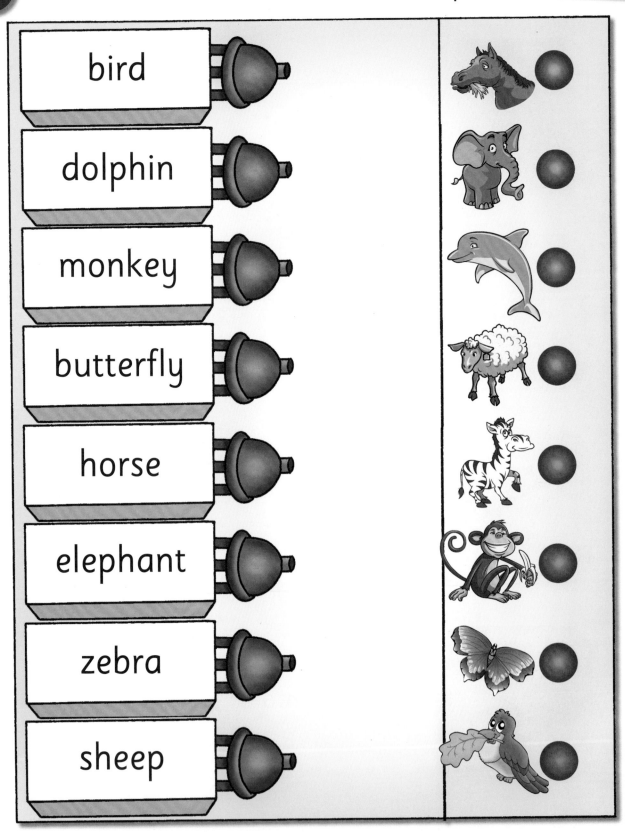

bird

dolphin

monkey

butterfly

horse

elephant

zebra

sheep

2 Who lives here?

fish
dolphin
dog
bird

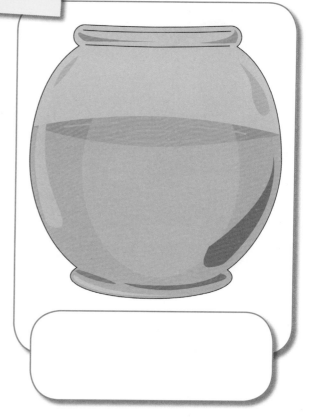

1 Match each picture to a word.

tail

eye

fire

wing

dragon

claws

2 What is it? Write the word.

3 Complete each sentence with a word.

 I can see a _____ tail.

 I can see _____ spikes.

 I can see _____ fire.

 I can see a _____ dragon.

4 to make a pattern.

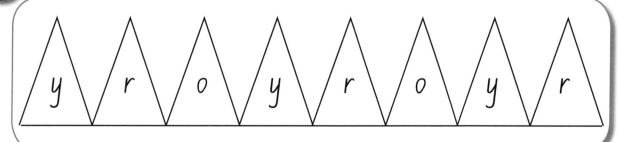

y r o y r o y r

Fun spot 3

22

1 Find Words. dolphin = **blue**, dragon = **red**,
butterfly = **purple**, dinosaur = **green**,
elephant = **grey**, monkey = **orange**

d	o	l	p	h	i	n	m	o	n	k	e	y
b	u	t	t	e	r	f	l	y	h	y	m	e
a	r	e	d	r	a	g	o	n	u	t	h	s
e	l	e	p	h	a	n	t	e	s	a	i	d
y	o	u	d	i	n	o	s	a	u	r	m	e
m	o	n	k	e	y	d	r	a	g	o	n	e
h	l	m	b	u	t	t	e	r	f	l	y	d
d	i	n	o	s	a	u	r	n	j	k	r	z
p	r	e	h	a	d	o	l	p	h	i	n	x
e	l	e	p	h	a	n	t	s	r	c	b	n
d	r	a	g	o	n	m	o	n	k	e	y	o
i	b	u	t	t	e	r	f	l	y	h	d	a
q	v	d	i	n	o	s	a	u	r	b	c	z

22

2 Which sense are they using?

see

hear

smell

touch

taste

1 Make word families. Complete each word.

eg words

 _p_eg

 __eg

 __eg

 __eg

Hi, I am Eggster.

et words

 _n_et

 __et

 __et

 __et

 __et

Hi, I am Jet Set.

ell words

 __ell

 __ell

 __ell

 ___ell

 __ell

 ___ell

en words

 _p_en

 __en

 __en

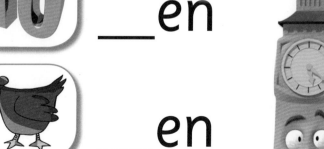 __en

Ding dong!
I am
Big Ben.

25

1 Match each word to a number.

one

four

two

seven

1

2

3

4

5

6

7

five

six

three

2 Trace.

3 Help Meg set the table. Draw seven hats, cups and bags. Draw candles on the cake.

Happy Birthday
Meg
Meg is 7 today

Fun spot 4

1 Find the matching story characters.

2 Draw a line from each food to its food group.

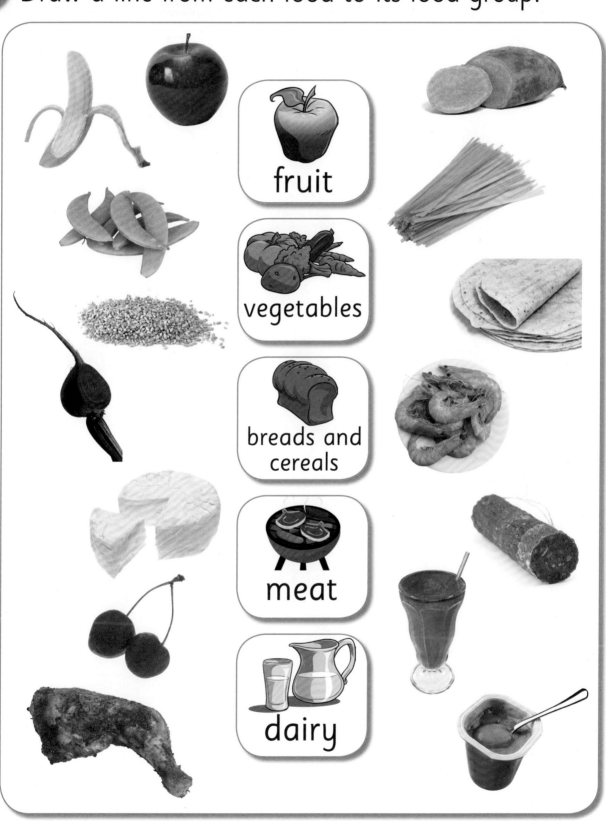

the star ⭐ if you can read the word.

come	play	my	now
yellow	red	purple	orange
here	seven	down	birthday
where	when	want	who

ABC Reading eggs

Days

day

Monday

Tuesday

Wednesday

Thursday

Friday

Saturday

Sunday

Animals

dolphin

monkey

zebra

elephant

hen

rabbit

sheep

butterfly

WOW!

You have finished Level 2.
Here's a trophy for you.

has successfully completed Level 2
of ABC Reading Eggs.

You are an excellent reader and writer.